DEMOCRACY AND SELF-ORGANIZATION

DEMOCRACY AND SELF-ORGANIZATION
THE CHANGE OF WHICH BARACK OBAMA SPEAKS

ROBERT AZIZ

To those who have awakened

to the exigencies of 21st century democratic process

CONTENTS

INTRODUCTION

Much as individuals have destinies, countries and even cultures do as well. Now such destinies should not be conceived of as preordained or fixed paths. Rather, they exist as developmental potentials which life at its depths invariably calls us toward, while ultimately making it a matter of our ethical fortitude as to whether we will embrace or abandon them.

For some 20 years, through my work as a psychoanalytical therapist, scholarly author and executive mentor within the business sector, I have been a devout student of our cultural problem of meaning and destiny. Having taken as my starting point the works of Sigmund Freud and C. G. Jung, which have been at the forefront of our cultural discussion of this problem for the past 100 years, most recently, I introduced an altogether new theoretical model within the area of the psychology of the unconscious, which I have termed the *Syndetic Paradigm*.[1]

The Syndetic Paradigm holds that all of life, which is to say, nature in its entirety, is bound together in process, a complex process of spontaneous self-organization. Inwardly and outwardly, in other words, individually and collectively, we are cease-lessly and unconditionally subject to the purposive, progressive and thus innately moral directives of self-organizing nature. It has been my conclusion that understanding ourselves and our lives in terms of self-organizing dynamics is the destiny to which we are now called. It has been my further conclusion that only by way of our knowledge of this destiny will we uncover the reasons for the powerful, but to date largely unexplained, collective attraction to a vision for change that is most certainly positioned on the forefront of this cultural realignment. I am referring to the political, social and cultural vision of Senator Barack Obama.

The theoretical progression from the Freudian to the Jung-ian to the Syndetic understanding of the psyche and its dynamics is something to which we must give at least brief consideration. In contrast to the Freudian conflict model, wherein the conscious and unconscious are completely at odds with each other and thus eter-nally battle for supremacy, within the Jungian model the uncon-scious is understood to support or regulate the psyche as a whole, which is to say, spontaneously bring about its self-organization. Now although the Jungian model of self-regulation or sponta-neous self-organization remained to all intents and purposes an internal model or what I refer to as a *closed-system* model, Jung was most certainly given glimpses of other possibilities. Based on his study of dream symbols, which he took to refer not just to the personality of the subject, as they typically would be believed to do, but to parallel events in the external world, Jung formulated the *synchronicity theory.* For different reasons, however, not the least of which being the late date of its formulation—Jung was in his mid-seventies and his closed-system model had become entrenched after over forty years of development and revision—the synchronicity theory would remain something of a theoretical anomaly within the Jungian Paradigm's closed-system model. The Syndetic Paradigm, by contrast, after twenty years of theoretical and clinical work on synchronicity and its implications, has taken the critical theoretical step of moving from a closed-system model of a self-regulatory psyche to an open-system model of a psyche in a self-organizing totality. Since the mid-1980s, I should further note, the significance of self-organization for such diverse disciplines as physics, psychology, politics, biology, evolution and economics has been scientifically pursued under the relatively new field of study termed *complexity theory.*

No doubt for most people the existence of self-organizing dynamics along the lines of which I am speaking seems altogether improbable, yet I would in turn ask for a calculation of the probability of the following. What is the probability, leaving aside for the moment the meaning, of a relatively young black man becoming the Democratic candidate for President? What is the probability of a black presidential candidate whose first name rhymes with the name of the country in which America is engaged in a war, which the majority of Americans today wish they had never entered; whose last name rhymes with the first name of the individual to whom the 9/11 attacks have been attributed; and if that doesn't push enough buttons for the American voter, whose middle name is the surname of that country's former ruler whose purported activities became the justification for entering the war the majority of Americans today wish they had never entered? You would not need a doctorate in statistics to say the probability is low. Barack Obama himself was more than aware of the odds: "I was told," Obama recalls, "people will remember your name and won't like it. You can have one African name, but not two. You can be Barack Smith or Joe Obama—but not Barack Obama."[2] How about Barack Hussein Obama? Given then this extremely low probability, I would in turn offer with reference to the question of the meaning of this appellative pattern—which is to say, with reference to the compensatory message self-organizing nature is here presenting— it would seem to have something to do with the need to overcome our cultural attachment to what I have termed *false absolutes*. We will return to the problem of false absolutes later.

The principle and even general idea of spontaneous self-organization is outside the experience of most people. Yet, if we were for a moment to think about it, would it not be the case that democracy is its political correlate? Would it not be the case that to believe in the principle of democracy would be to believe in the ability of a people within a whole system to spontaneously self-organize, thereby furthering not only themselves, but also the total system of which they are part? To believe in democracy is to have unconditional faith in the consciousness and self-organizing capabilities of people. But having said this, we recognize that the self-organizing dynamics of democracy will in practice be restricted, if not obstructed altogether, in the absence of a process to support them functionally. Here, however, we venture into sensitive territory; for to the extent people would regard democracy as an ideal rather than as a process, they would view democracy as something of which they are categorically in possession, rather than something they must actively pursue, refine and protect. But surely, they would at least concede that the often-stated criticisms of the *politics* of our culture are no less criticisms of its democratic process.

"One of the toughest things about being a senator," Barack Obama told Charlie Rose in 2006 with reference to the lack of true legislative process, "is most of the time you can't punch the box that says 'none of the above.'"[3] For democracy to be functional, its process must be inclusive and dynamic. For democracy to be functional, it must hold open the requisite space for the genuine processing of information. For democracy to be functional, everyone must be invested in the outcome of the self-organizing process and no individual or group should experience the paralyzing apathy of marginalization. All important and critical issues must be put on the table and openly and frankly processed, not only by the voting public, but also no less by their elected representatives. Democracy would, in this regard, be a truly inclusive and dynamic process altogether freed from the narrow, self-serving agendas and manipulations of power politics and lobbyists. "I am in this race," Barack Obama told a Des Moines, Iowa audience in 2007, "to tell the corporate lobbyists, that their days of setting the agenda in Washington are over … they will not drown out the voices of the American people when I am President."[4] Elsewhere, he wrote: "Most political scientists would probably disagree with me, but to my mind, there's a difference between a corporate lobby whose clout is based on money alone, and a group of like-minded individuals … coming together to promote their interests; between those who use their economic power to magnify their political influence far beyond what their numbers might justify, and those who are simply seeking to pool their votes to sway their representatives. The former subvert the very idea of democracy. The latter are its essence."[5] Finally, and perhaps above all else, in contrast to the culture of fear so characteristic of the post-9/11 period in which the freedom of individual thought and self-expression has succumbed to manufactured compliance, a functional democratic process must be a system in which its guarantors understand that in the absence of an individual having the right to think and in turn openly process those thoughts with others the democratic right to vote means little or nothing.

Now as much as self-organizing nature leads us to choices that benefit us both individually and collectively, our psyches are not without regressive tendencies that would have us do otherwise. In fact if this were not the case there would be no question of everyone going straight to enlightenment. Self-organizing process, therefore, needs to be as much protected in terms of its psychological dynamics, which is to say, in terms of its intrapsychic dynamics, as it needs to be protected outwardly by the safeguards of our political process.

A significant intrapsychic obstruction to self-organizing process is the human propensity to create and engage life through *false absolutes*. People love to categorize, but it is when their tendencies to oversimplify and concretize meanings combine that things become problematic. What is at once the appeal and problem of false absolutes is that people derive from them a sense of, yet far more accurately put, illusion of certainty and control. In *The Syndetic Paradigm*, I write the following about false absolutes and false certainties:

> The vulnerability of humanity to false absolutes, which are, so to speak, the by-products of concretized or fixed forms, is a most frightening vulnerability indeed. Whether they are of a religious, psychological, social or political nature, when it comes to the workings of the human psyche, false absolutes are tremendously seductive. The reason for this, it seems to me, is perhaps to be found in the linkage that exists in the minds of human beings between the search for meaning and the need for certainty. We would not be pressed to imagine that one of the drivers at the very core of our search for meaning is our no less instinctive need for certainty. Far less apparent, though, would be the reason why these closely related drives might end up being altogether at odds with each other. How is it that certainty and meaning so suddenly

diverge from their parallel trajectories? The answer, to my mind, is that certainty may very well be acquired for a far cheaper price than that which must be paid when truth and meaning are obtained along with it. Certainty may be entirely manufactured by ego control and as such have little, if anything, to do with truth and meaning. Certainty may be an utter fabrication of ego control and as such have nothing whatsoever to do with Reality. Certainty of this particular sort, therefore, having everything to do with ego control and power and nothing to do with meaning, is most appropriately termed *false certainty. Concretized or fixed forms lead to false absolutes, which in turn produce false certainties.*[6]

One of the key arguments of *The Syndetic Paradigm* is that in order for our culture to find its way to an experience of meaning commensurate with the developmental path to which we are called by self-organizing nature, we must break our addictive pattern of substituting one exhausted and failing false absolute for another and move to a direct encounter with life in process. We must, in other words, allow dynamic meaning to present directly to us through the process of self-organizing life unencumbered. Here our engagement with self-organizing nature becomes not so much a question of what we need to do, but rather, what we need not to do. And what we especially need not to do is subject self-organizing nature and its process to the restrictions of false categorizations.

Much to the inconvenience of Barack Obama's political adversaries, who have sought either to discredit or inconspicuously emulate him, or both, the change of which Barack Obama speaks is no easy target. It is no easy target, I would suggest, because it is operating outside prevailing cultural assumptions about what politicians should say, especially when they are campaigning for office. The change of which Barack Obama speaks is no easy target because it is not so much about this or that specific idea or solution, but rather, about the *how* we are to get to this or that specific idea or solution. The change of which Barack Obama speaks is above all else about *process*.

As indicated at the outset of this treatise, it is not just Barack Obama's adversaries who struggle to understand this shift. Indeed even though many of his supporters intuit the change of which he speaks is authentically new and different and as such of great political and cultural significance, they nonetheless are at a loss to anticipate its specific direction. This discrepancy is not surprising in light of the nature and extent of the shift in question.

It would have been of no small significance to Caroline Kennedy and her uncle Senator Edward Kennedy, the only surviving child and brother, respectively, of the late President John F. Kennedy that American University in Washington D.C. was chosen as the place for their endorsements of Barack Obama; for it was at that same university John Kennedy gave his brilliant and impassioned speech on world peace. And it was, furthermore, of no small significance that Caroline Kennedy, who as a young girl suffered the loss of her father in service to his country as President, would have not only personalized the words of her endorsement to the extent she did, but situated them within the context of our current cultural crisis of meaning. "It's a special privilege," Caroline Kennedy offered those in attendance as a prelude to her endorsement, "to come to American University where President Kennedy made his immortal call for a peaceful world—a world made safe for diversity—a world that cherishes our children's future. Over the years, I've been deeply moved by the people who've told me they wish they could feel inspired and hopeful about America the way people did when my father was president. The longing is even more profound today. Fortunately, there is one candidate who offers that same sense of hope and inspiration and I am proud to endorse Senator Barack Obama for President."[7]

Some forty-five years previous at American University, John Kennedy, it is important for the purposes of our discussion to understand, unequivocally demonstrated his faith in and commitment to the self-organizing capabilities of humanity as a whole— the self-organizing capabilities of humanity to create, by way of an inclusive, process-based engagement and dialogue, not just a lasting peace, but also, its necessary attendant condition, a better world for everyone. "What kind of peace," John Kennedy rhetorically asked his audience,

do I mean? What kind of peace do we seek? Not a Pax

Americana enforced on the world by American weapons of war. Not the peace of the grave or the security of the slave. I am talking about genuine peace, the kind of peace that makes life on earth worth living, the kind that enables men and nations to grow and to hope and to build a better life for their children—not merely peace for Americans but peace for all men and women—not merely peace in our time but peace for all time … There is no single, simple key to this peace—no grand or magic formula to be adopted by one or two powers. Genuine peace must be the product of many nations, the sum of many acts. It must be dynamic, not static, changing to meet the challenge of each new generation. For peace is a process—a way of solving problems.[8]

Of course it is the *how* of the peace of which John Kennedy speaks that especially intrigues: firstly, because of its alignment with that to which we have been called by our cultural destiny—inclusivity, process and self-organization; secondly, because it is now the case, after a forty-five year hiatus, that an individual by way of his unique life and political journey has inclined the gaze of the American people, perhaps even the gaze of the people of the world as a whole, to return to a destiny that has yet to be fulfilled. The endorsement of Caroline Kennedy, I will yet again reiterate, is of no small significance.

What Barack Obama's and John Kennedy's visions for social and political change for America and the world have in common is their alignment with three fundamental assumptions of the new paradigm of which I have spoken. Those assumptions are as follows: inclusivity, which is to say, everything and everyone are bound together in process and must be engaged and cared for as such; the capability of whole systems to spontaneously self-organize; that spontaneous self-organization will be restricted, if not altogether arrested, as a result of the imposition of false absolutes.

The false absolutes to which I am referring and to which we will now turn fall into three categories: 1) the imposition of false absolutes pertaining to individual or collective ideals, especially to the extent identification with those ideals compromises individual or collective capabilities to self-reflect; 2) the imposition of false absolutes pertaining to secular or religious ideologies; 3) the imposition of false absolutes in a manner that would lessen or obstruct the engagement in process of an individual as a human being, first and foremost.

I

FALSE ABSOLUTES AND IDEALS

Ideals are typically not of this world, but rather, that toward which the people of this world aspire. Accordingly, even though most individuals hold ideals about themselves, and others in turn project ideals onto them, seldom, if ever, do the actual and ideal directly align. Such discrepancies notwithstanding, there remains, however, no shortage of individuals who choose to imagine otherwise. Of course what I have just explained applies no less to the collective consciousness of a nation. As with an individual, a nation may also hold an idealized picture of itself with the subsequent discrepancy between the ideal and the actual being no less problematic. How exactly is it problematic? The answer is twofold. Firstly, to the extent an individual or the collective consciousness of a nation identifies with a wished-for or idealized picture of self, as opposed to the actual one, the individual or nation will be under the influence of a false absolute and by extension of that a false certainty. Secondly, to the extent an individual or the collective consciousness of a nation identifies with a false absolute in the form of a wished-for or idealized picture of self, as opposed to the actual one, the individual or nation will be incapable of self-reflec-

tion. The upshot of either scenario being the individual or nation
will be altogether disconnected in process from self-organizing nature. To be in process, by contrast, means the challenges of the actual are not concealed by the wished-for or imagined; it means real
frustrations—healthy feelings that would compel an individual or
nation to make things better—are not anaesthetized by escape into
the false comfort of a false certainty; it means an individual or nation would not be so identified with an idealized sense of self that
the capability to self-reflect is altogether lost.

In *The Audacity of Hope* Barack Obama offers a remarkably
insightful account of the human propensity to escape into the illusory comfort of false certainties. Writing with reference to the
charm that so characterized the presidency of Ronald Reagan and
the sway it held over both individual and collective experience,
Barack Obama relates:

> as unconvinced as I might have been by his John Wayne,
> *Father Knows Best* pose, his policy by anecdote, and his
> gratuitous assaults on the poor, I understood his appeal.
> It was the same appeal that the military bases back in Ha-
> waii had always held for me as a young boy, with their
> tidy streets and well-oiled machinery, the crisp uniforms
> and crisper salutes. It was related to the pleasure I still
> get from watching a well-played baseball game, or my
> wife gets from watching reruns of *The Dick Van Dyke Show*.
> Reagan spoke to America's longing for order, our need to

believe that we are not simply subject to blind, impersonal forces ... Reagan may have exaggerated the sins of the welfare state, and certainly liberals were right to complain that his domestic policies tilted heavily toward economic elites, with corporate raiders making tidy profits throughout the eighties while unions were busted and the income of the average working stiff flatlined.

Nevertheless, by promising to side with those who worked hard, obeyed the law, cared for their families, and loved their country, Reagan offered Americans a sense of a common purpose that liberals seemed no longer able to muster.[9]

The vulnerability of humanity to false absolutes and false certainties, I will again say, is a most frightening vulnerability. Frightening because false absolutes and false certainties developmentally incapacitate both individuals and nations. False absolutes and false certainties incapacitate to the extent they keep us from engaging in process the deeper work upon which our inspired individual and collective destinies can only be built. Accordingly, as Barack Obama himself would not fail to observe, the simplistic yet well-packaged optimism of the Reagan years would not presage a more conscious and caring America, but rather, serve as the stepping-stones to a dark agenda[10] that would directly exploit humanity's vulnerability to false absolutes and false certainties. We will return to this problem in the section dealing with false absolutes and ideologies.

It is unfortunately the case that identifying with a false absolute has far greater appeal for most people than the less tidy and even painful work of self-reflection and developmental process. Simplistic answers, to be sure, are much preferred to the hard work of genuine process, even though the best solutions never come from the former. Of course we can readily deduce from this that democratic process would be strengthened if its political leadership were to establish ethical parameters that would eschew the exploitation of such human vulnerabilities. Democracy, in this respect, would be well served if its leadership would take as its ethical task the responsibility to inform rather than misinform and manipulate. It would be well served if its leadership would treat as sacred its commitment to an open and candid democratic process, rather than shamelessly appealing to the base sentiments of its populace. "The pursuit of peace," John Kennedy told his American University audience with reference to the leadership challenge of circumventing these very human limitations, "is not as dramatic as the pursuit of war—and frequently the words of the pursuer fall on deaf ears. But we have no more urgent task."[11]

If democratic leadership is to be worthy of its designation, it has a responsibility to afford its people the opportunity to think and make choices. It has a responsibility to afford its people the opportunity to make informed choices about the complex and genuinely pressing, as opposed to the simplistic and contrived. To lead others, in this respect, can only mean to educate, as President

Franklin Delano Roosevelt held. "Democracy cannot succeed," FDR notably believed, "unless those who express their choice are prepared to choose wisely. The real safeguard of democracy, therefore, is education."[12]

Democratic leadership must take as its responsibility the task of bringing about by way of education and process, political, social and cultural directions that will endure. Such leadership of course would require a great deal of anyone who would aspire to it. It would require a strong and differentiated personality. It would require an individual to hold the course even in the absence of collective approval, rather than succumb to what I have technically termed *externalization*. It would require an individual to hold the course much as Barack Obama himself did when he stood in opposition to the war with Iraq during a time when it was regarded by most as unpatriotic to do so. It would require an individual to hold the course against the otherwise overwhelming strength of the frighteningly unconscious current of collective opinion. "An externalized individual," I explain in *The Syndetic Paradigm* with reference to the challenge of political leadership,

> can never be a genuine leader, although certainly many such individuals have found their way into positions of leadership. Externalized leaders do not shape public opinion as such, rather they obtain and hold power by discerning where the parade of collective opinion is heading and then, as quickly as possible, making a hopefully clandes-

tine dash to its front. 'There are only two kinds of political leaders,' Jim Coutts relates by way of placing in context the uniqueness of the leadership of the former Canadian Prime Minister, Pierre Elliott Trudeau, 'those who want to be somebody, and those who want to do something. To the former,' Coutts continues, 'the challenge is to get to the top and to stay there; to the latter, the challenge is to bring about reform.' Whereas the 'leadership' of the former, we would add, is about the pursuit of power as an end in itself, and as such stands strictly within the realm of ego control, the leadership of the latter, by contrast, has its basis in ego strength. Whereas the 'leadership' of the former is about being shaped by the prevailing collective opinion; the leadership of the latter is about contributing to the shaping of it.[13]

Standing up to the powerful current of collective opinion is no easy task; changing its direction is all the harder, for what may be required to bring about collective self-reflection is the breaking down of the very false absolutes derived from ideals with which the collective to its detriment is identified. It makes sense that those who will speak most forcefully to the problems presented by such false absolutes will be individuals of moral fortitude who have come to know, through their own life experiences and the life experiences of others they have observed firsthand, what it means to live on the wrong side of a collectively held ideal. Reverend Dr.

Martin Luther King was such an individual and he was indeed uncompromising in reprimanding what he regarded as America's hubris—her inflationary identification with certain collectively held ideals that had remained unchallenged in light of her collective inability to self-reflect. "I love this country too much," Martin Luther King, the civil rights leader and 1964 Nobel Peace Prize laureate, told the congregates at Atlanta's Ebenezer Baptist Church on February 4th, 1968, "to see the drift that it has taken. God didn't call America to do what she's doing in the world now. God didn't call America to engage in a senseless, unjust war as the war in Vietnam. And we are criminals in that war. We've committed more war crimes almost than any other nation in the world, and I'm going to continue to say it. And we won't stop it because of our pride and our arrogance as a nation."[14]

False absolutes and false certainties developmentally incapacitate both individuals and nations. False absolutes and false certainties developmentally incapacitate to the extent they keep us from engaging in process the deeper work upon which our inspired individual and collective destinies can only be built. By way of false absolutes and false certainties, individuals or the collective consciousnesses of nations effectively become *dissociated*, which is to say, they become psychologically split or fragmented, divided within themselves. C. G. Jung, who was well aware of these dynamics, in both their personal and collective forms, was greatly concerned about their implications for political process. To the extent the psyche of an individual or the collective consciousness of

a nation becomes split in this manner, the inferior and even con-
temptible part that disappears off the radar screen of consciousness will become part of what Jung terms the *shadow*. Once situated within the shadow those rejected components of the personality or collective consciousness will continue to grow and operate
unchecked by consciousness, which is to say, without the benefit of
any self-reflection whatsoever. As a consequence, they remain in
an altogether unredeemed and unredeemable state only presenting themselves to the world in the form of projections unleashed
on other individuals, groups or nations. Writing about this problem with specific reference to the Cold War tensions between the
West and the then Soviet Union, Jung, in a work completed only
ten days before his death, explained:

> Our world is, so to speak, dissociated like a neurotic, with
> the Iron Curtain marking the symbolic line of division.
> Western man, becoming aware of the aggressive will to
> power of the East, sees himself forced to take extraordi-
> nary measures of defense, at the same time as he prides
> himself on his virtue and good intentions.
>
> What he fails to see is that it is his own vices, which
> he has covered up by good international manners, that are
> thrown back in his face by the communist world, shame-
> lessly and methodically. What the West has tolerated, but
> secretly and with a slight sense of shame (the diplomatic
> lie, systematic deception, veiled threats), comes back into

the open and in full measure from the East and ties us up in neurotic knots. It is the face of his own evil shadow that grins at Western man from the other side of the Iron Curtain.

It is a state of affairs that explains the peculiar feeling of helplessness of so many people in Western societies. They have begun to realize that the difficulties confronting us are moral problems, and that the attempts to answer them by a policy of piling up nuclear arms or by economic 'competition' is achieving little, for it cuts both ways.[15]

If peace, as we saw John Kennedy himself assert, is in fact a process then it follows that our identification with a false absolute and false certainty in the form of a concretized collective ideal most undoubtedly presents an obstruction to peace. Our capability to see through and shatter such concretized ideals by way of collective self-reflection constitutes, by contrast, our greatest strength. In keeping, therefore, with Martin Luther King's admonishment of the idealized and thus false sense of goodness that made America unrepentant in her pursuit of a "senseless, unjust war as the war in Vietnam," in keeping with C. G. Jung's indictment of the role played by the West's own shadow under the cover of "good international manners" during the Cold War, John Kennedy, in speaking to his audience at American University about world peace, would offer no false comfort concerning yet another concretized ideal of American goodness. Speaking directly about the negative consequences to world peace of the discrepancy between the collectively held American ideal of freedom and justice and the actuality of America's yet to be resolved civil rights issues, and doing so, we should further note, at a time when opposition within his own country to what he was saying was not to be underestimated, John Kennedy told his audience:

> Finally, my fellow Americans, let us examine our attitude toward peace and freedom here at home. The quality and spirit of our own society must justify and support our efforts abroad. We must show it in the dedication of our own lives ... we must all, in our daily lives, live up to the age-old faith that peace and freedom walk together. In too many of our cities today, the peace is not secure because freedom is incomplete.
>
> It is the responsibility of the executive branch at all levels of government—local, State, and National—to provide and protect that freedom for all of our citizens by all means within their authority. It is the responsibility of the legislative branch at all levels, wherever that authority is not now adequate, to make it adequate. And it is the responsibility of all citizens in all sections of this country to respect the rights of all others and to respect the law of the land.
>
> All this is not unrelated to world peace. 'When a man's ways please the Lord,' the Scriptures tell us, 'he

maketh even his enemies to be at peace with him.' And is not peace, in the last analysis, basically a matter of human rights—the right to live out our lives without fear of devastation—the right to breathe air as nature provided it—the right of future generations to a healthy existence?[16]

Progressive change does not occur by way of our engagement in process with illusions. Progressive change, rather, proceeds by way of our engagement in process with that which is real. To be transformed by life necessitates the bringing of our genuine selves to life. To be transformed by way of self-reflection, either as individuals or in terms of the collective consciousness of which we are part, necessitates the bringing of that which we individually or collectively are into the process of self-reflection. How can self-organizing process transform that which it cannot directly touch? How can self-organizing process support our transformation if all that we present to it are self-deceptions, false absolutes and false certainties—if all that we present to it are highly idealized and altogether false representations of our individual or collective goodness? "A method of meditation or a form of contemplation," the Trappist contemplative Thomas Merton wrote, and into which we should now insert the word *self-reflection*,

that merely produces the illusion of having 'arrived somewhere,' of having achieved security and preserved one's familiar status by playing a part, will eventually have to

be unlearned in dread—or else we will be confirmed in the
arrogance, the impenetrable self-assurance of the Pharisee.
We will become impervious to the deepest truths. We will
be closed to all who do not participate in our illusion. ... In
order to avoid apparent evil, this pseudo-goodness will ignore the summons of genuine good. It will prefer routine
duty to courage and creativity. In the end it will be content
with established procedures and safe formulas, while turning a blind eye to the greatest enormities of injustice and
uncharity.[17]

To be under the influence of a false absolute in the form
of an idealized sense of goodness is to cut ourselves off from the
transformative dynamics of self-organizing process. It is to put
ourselves at odds not only with the process of our own individual
and collective journeys by way of self-organizing nature, but it is
to place ourselves on equally unproductive paths in our relations
with other nations, especially those with whom we are in conflict.
False absolutes and false certainties in the form of collective ideals
blindfold us; and the presence of such blindfolds does not make for
good foreign policy. Good foreign policy, by contrast, requires clarity of vision—a clarity of vision in which the *inward* is held, by way
of individual and collective self-reflection, as sharply in focus as
the *outward*. The following passage from the classic Chinese philo-
sophical text the *Tao Te Ching* speaks to this very point. I would
especially draw attention to the following: firstly, the text cautions

against premature, which is to say, unreflective or unconscious action—something the contentious *preemptive doctrine* of the Bush administration, I would add, makes all the more difficult to keep in check; secondly, it tells us that in contrast to the crass, in-your-face dynamics characterizing the way of power, actions informed by self-reflection and thus at one with self-organizing dynamics have the appearance of being *non-actions*; thirdly and finally, we see that the philosophy of the text, being altogether adaptable to actual conditions, acknowledges there indeed are times in which war may be unavoidable. The text reads:

> There is a saying among soldiers:
> I dare not make the first move but would rather play the guest;
> I dare not advance an inch but would rather withdraw a foot.

> This is called marching without appearing to move,
> Rolling up your sleeves without showing your arm,
> Capturing the enemy without attacking,
> Being armed without weapons.

> There is no greater catastrophe than underestimating the enemy.
> By underestimating the enemy, I almost lose what I value.

Therefore when the battle is joined,

The underdog [or he who deplores the situation[18]] will

win.[19]

Something of which we should be sure concerning the
above text—the Chinese origins of which have been attributed to
the 6th century BC—is that it is anything but an ungrounded piece
of idealistic philosophy. The text, as already noted, is not about
the avoidance of wars that must be fought; rather it is about the
avoidance of wars that need not happen. It is about uncovering
opportunities to de-escalate, rather than escalate international tensions. It is about finding and supporting sustainable solutions to
international conflicts, as opposed to the opportunistic pursuit of
short-term return. It is about stopping those projection-driven political and military initiatives that historically have authored far
too many otherwise avoidable catastrophes including America's
most recent war in Iraq. It is about holding firm against the seduc-
tive pull of false absolutes and false certainties, especially those
stemming from collective ideals of goodness.

Was it not sorrowfully the case that once the original and
ultimately groundless justification for war with Iraq had been exposed the collective-idealism card was played and exploited? Was
it not the case that no sooner had the supposed WMD threat to the
world been proven to be unfounded then the collective consciousness of democratic culture was knocked senseless yet again by way
of the manipulation of its idealized sense of goodness? Was it not

then claimed that Saddam needed to be overthrown because the brutality of his dictatorship was an affront to the values of democratic culture? Unreflectively received, there can be no doubt this assertion struck a chord. Today, however, seeing the horrific toll on both sides of that war and weighing objectively for the first time its cost, human and otherwise, the grand tally of which is still far from settled, we are more than inclined to ask ourselves if sufficient individual and collective self-reflection preceded the taking of military action. How numbed was democratic culture by the false absolutes of collective goodness? How great was the hubris of democratic culture that it could comfortably speak of the taking of even one innocent life under the euphemistic, near-divine phrasing, *shock and awe*? How could our false sense of collective goodness—we must know if we are to learn anything of value about ourselves from this—have categorically prohibited even the exploration of productive alternatives to war and its horrific attendant conditions?

Saddam was a dictator, but how opportune it was to forget that he was encouraged, financially supported and armed by democratic nations during years of his rule that were far more brutal than those at the time of his overthrow. When it was of benefit to democratic nations to do so, Saddam was given a pass. The incontrovertible fact remains that democratic culture has supported and used dictators like Saddam to its advantage; and to this day continues to do so. The incontrovertible truth is that democratic culture has supported and used dictators like Saddam without any

regard whatsoever for the suffering of those living under their rule
and without regard for the long-term implications of such support
to the world order. "Because of the enormity of the Soviet threat,"
Barack Obama writes with reference to foreign policy transgres-
sions of the past, "… American policy makers came to view nation-
alist movements, ethnic struggles, reform efforts, or left-leaning
policies anywhere in the world through the lens of the Cold War—
potential threats they felt outweighed our professed commitment
to freedom and democracy. For decades we would tolerate and
even aid thieves like Mobutu, thugs like Noriega, so long as they
opposed communism. Occasionally U.S. covert operations would
engineer the removal of democratically elected leaders in countries
like Iran—with seismic repercussions that haunt us to this day."[20]
As an addendum to this we should mention that it was in fact the
perceived threat posed by Iran's Islamic Revolution under Aya-
tollah Khomeini that led America under President Ronald Reagan
and other democratic nations to increase significantly their diplo-
matic, financial and military support of Saddam and his regime.

Perhaps, prior to the invasion of Iraq, if the vision of democratic culture could have been disentangled from the false absolute of collective goodness—which led democratic culture to arm
and support a dictator and then in turn "solve" the problem of
his dictatorship without regard for its own very significant role in
the whole problem—it would have been able to see and engage in
process, not the illusory, but rather, reality itself, thereby making
decisions commensurate with the ethics of democratic culture. If

democratic culture had just done the authentically good thing and figured into the Saddam equation the reality of its own demons and its own shadow, much as John Kennedy laid bare to the then Soviet Union and the world the imperfections and shortcomings of America's civil rights struggle to achieve its unrealized, yet defining dream of dignity and freedom for all, it may have found its way, as the *Tao Te Ching* tells us, to "capturing the enemy without attacking" thereby opening space for genuinely productive courses of action, genuinely productive alternatives to war.

A dramatic advance in consciousness occurs when by way of self-reflection and knowledge of our individual or collective shadows we shift from it being a question of *their* problem to it being a question of *our* problem. A dramatic advance in consciousness occurs when we actually place ourselves within the same circle as those with whom we are in conflict. Now it is important to realize that standing with an individual or nation in such a circle is in itself not to be construed as a condoning of the offensive conduct of the other. Even if one were to go so far as to feel compassion for an individual or nation with whom one was in conflict—and the more deeply one looks at one's individual or collective shadow the more likely that is to happen—would not be to condone the other's offensive conduct. When, for instance, John Kennedy acknowledged to the world, with reference to America's struggling civil rights movement that "[in] too many of our cities today, the peace is not secure because freedom is incomplete," he was certainly not at the same time condoning what he knew to be serious civil rights failings in the Soviet Union. "As Americans," John Kennedy quite plainly stated to his audience at American University, "we find communism profoundly repugnant as a negation of personal freedom and dignity."[21] In contrast, therefore, to the conclusions of the more absolutistic-minded, to *identify with*, is not to condone, nor is it indicative of weakness; to *identify with*, rather, is indicative of strength and insight. For John Kennedy to have gone so far as to acknowledge that the United States and the Soviet Union had their respective shortcomings when it came to the securing of the civil rights of their citizens, for John Kennedy to have placed the civil rights challenges of the United States and Soviet Union within a common circle, was to lead from strength; it was to lead, not just one country, but both countries beyond the false absolutes, false certainties and the altogether contrived exclusivity attending idealized goodness into the dynamic meaning, inclusivity and reality-based processing of self-organizing nature.

The formal drawing of such inclusive circles, which are the necessary precursors of all genuine peace negotiations, require either exceptional vision and strength on the part of a leader within one of the parties concerned or the intervention of an equally conscious and determined third party to hold open the requisite space within which the peace process can unfold. Certainly this is something former President Jimmy Carter, the 2002 Nobel Peace Prize laureate has come to experience first hand in light of his concerted efforts of late to reopen peace negotiations in the Middle East. Although the Palestinian/Israeli conflict continues to be arguably the most destabilizing unresolved problem, not only for the Middle East, but the world as a whole, no peace negotiations have occurred since the year 2000. Peace needs a process, yet in light of the complexity of this particular conflict the parties concerned have not been able to make their way into a common circle. The only hope for peace, Jimmy Carter has unwaveringly held, is for the United States to resume its position as an honest broker and initiator of genuine dialogue and process. Writing with reference to the need for a third party of vision and strength to create and hold open to the Israelis and Palestinians the requisite space for self-organizing process and peace, Jimmy Carter reflects:

> It has always been clear that the antagonists cannot be expected to take the initiative to resolve their own differences. Hatred and distrust in the Middle East are too ingrained and pride is too great for any of the disputing parties to offer invitations or concessions that they know will almost inevitably be rejected. Accommodation must be sought through negotiation with all parties to the dispute, with each having fair representation and the right to participate in free discussions. Compromise is necessary from both sides, with clear distinctions made between what their dreams and ideology dictate and what is pragmatically possible. ...
>
> Strong support for peace talks must come from the United States, preferably involving representatives of the

United Nations, the European Union, and Russia. Until recently, America's leaders were known and expected to exert maximum influence in an objective, nonbiased way to achieve peace in the Middle East.[22]

Inclusivity is indeed an operant condition of self-organization and as such an operant condition of life itself. History's most revered leaders, accordingly, are not those who separated and divided people and nations, but rather, those who brought together and united people and nations. I would go so far as to say the more inclusive and all-encompassing the concern and vision of a leader has been in this regard, collective esteem for that individual has increased and deepened proportionately. John Kennedy was such a leader; and although he held the highest office in his country, although he led the most powerful nation in the world, he did not exploit the power of his position to oppress. Rather, what John Kennedy offered, not only to all Americans, but the people of the world as a whole—those to whom he warmly and inclusively referred in his address to the 18th General Assembly of the United Nations on September 20th, 1963 as "my fellow inhabitants of this planet"[23]—were the noblest of human values and aspirations around which they could rally. "There's a final dimension to U.S. foreign policy," Barack Obama relates in *The Audacity of Hope*,

… that has less to do with avoiding war than promoting peace. The year I was born, President Kennedy stated in his inaugural address: 'To those people in the huts and villages of half the globe struggling to break the bonds of mass misery, we pledge our best efforts to help them help themselves, for whatever period is required—not because the Communists may be doing it, not because we seek their votes, but because it is right. If a free society cannot help the many who are poor, it cannot save the few who are rich.' Forty-five years later, that mass misery still exists. If we are to fulfill Kennedy's promise—and serve our long-term security interests—then we will have to go beyond a more prudent use of military force. We will have to align our policies to help reduce the spheres of insecurity, poverty, and violence around the world, and give more people a stake in the global order that has served us so well.[24]

I would like to add in bringing this section to a close that very much in contrast to the highly idealized, personality-centric leadership of the old paradigm, which is tantamount to a cult of personality, the leadership of the new paradigm has to do with the empowerment of others. "I like to think," Barack Obama told the *New Yorker* in 2006, "I have a message that's useful, I like to think that I can contribute, otherwise I wouldn't have written [*The Audacity of Hope*]. There's the question of whether I am the right messenger for whatever message that is. And that's not clear as well, because, like anybody in politics, I've got strengths and I've got weaknesses, both politically and substantively."[25] The way of the new paradigm has to do with the empowerment of others. It has to do with leadership that by example conducts others to a working understanding of self-organizing process. It is not, to be sure, about individual power, but about the collective, self-organizing capability of people, lest we continue along the ultimately unproductive and meaningless path of substituting one failing false absolute for another, which is to say, substituting the failing idealization of one politician for the wished-for, yet still unchallenged, idealization of another. In short, it is about the *we* in "Yes, we can."

II

FALSE ABSOLUTES AND IDEOLOGIES

In *The Syndetic Paradigm* I draw several conclusions pertaining to our cultural crisis of meaning it would benefit our present discussion to consider. These conclusions are as follows: firstly, by way of self-organizing nature there is an evolution of consciousness; secondly, as a consequence of nature's evolutionary strivings our deepest beings, having become, as it were, *false absolute intolerant*, seek depth meaning by way of direct encounters with *unfolding life in process*; thirdly, despite this reconfiguration within the depths of our beings, the vast majority of people, not being consciously aware of this shift and its implications, wrongly continue to reach for false absolutes, much as people will continue to crave foods to which they are allergic. Of course such altogether misguided pursuits of false absolutes and false certainties only serve to worsen the crisis of meaning by which those individuals are gripped. Below, I quote at length the relevant passage from *The Syndetic Paradigm*:

> The history of the secular and religious ideologies of humanity … is a legacy of having imposed on life,

through fixed or concretized form, false absolutes and false certainties; and the imposition on life, through fixed or concretized form, of false absolutes and false certainties is always an act of violation of the soul. Perhaps even up to one hundred years ago, this formula could have been believed in and lived with relative authenticity, in spite of its ultimate destructiveness. Today, however, it cannot. There truly is an evolution of consciousness and thus what falls within the range of acceptability in one age becomes, or is on its way to becoming, a virtually intolerable condition in the next. Perhaps this shift in consciousness coincides with the fact that today there is little margin for error. As never before in humanity's history, unconsciousness could now very well destroy everything, and do so within a matter of moments. Whether it is for this reason or other ones, what we do know—what is clearly indicated in the dreams and outward compensatory experiences of people today—is that in this our present age our deepest beings are rebelling against the legacy of concretization, false absolutes and false certainties. What we do know is that we no longer can accommodate ourselves to that old formula. Yet because, I would also add by way of caution, it is our deepest beings and not our conscious selves that have rebelled against the old, our conscious selves continue to reach for the solution in the wrong places and in the wrong forms, much as even Jung himself did. Accordingly, with each vain attempt to resolve this crisis with yet another fixed-form cure, with yet another false absolute, we are repeatedly subjected to that to which our deeper selves have now developed a near-allergic aversion. No solution, we should be assured, be it spiritual, psychological, social, or political will come from such folly. For the answer to our crisis of meaning, which is unlike anything that humanity has previously faced, will come, not by way of concretization, but rather by way of our direct and conscious access through dynamic meaning to unfolding Reality.[26]

The imposition on life of the fixed or concretized forms of secular and religious ideologies is always an act of violation of the soul to the extent fixed or concretized forms sever our individual or collective relationship to the very thing that animates our souls, that is they sever our direct relationship to life in process. Rather than opening to us the precise and highly complex workings of self-organizing nature by which we might come to know ourselves and meaningfully engage others, false absolutes and false certainties, derived from secular and religious ideologies, serve only to arrest and disconnect us from ourselves and others. False absolutes and false certainties serve only to create impenetrable walls—walls from behind which we smugly hide from authentic and thus transformative encounters with life in process. "Unlike dynamic meaning, which opens life to us, false certainty," I explain in *The Syndetic Paradigm*, "closes life off. False certainty provides

false comfort; it does not prod us forward into life and consciousness, as dynamic meaning can only do, at times gently and at times
not so gently. False certainty creates in us a type of tunnel vision,
thereby enabling us to ignore the real problems to which our development is most fully tied. False certainty may uplift our spirits,
but it will never heal them."[27]

False absolutes and false certainties will never heal our
spirits because they are incapable of bringing the transformative
energies of life directly to bear on what ails us. False absolutes and
false certainties will never heal us since they separate us from,
rather than lead us to, authentic and thus transformative encounters by way of self-organizing process with ourselves, others and
life as a whole. False absolutes, to be sure, will never be part of the
solution to what ails us; such absolutism, rather, is the problem.
Speaking with reference to the prevalence of absolutism within our
culture today, while at the same time suggesting practical steps to
counter it, Barack Obama told *Newsweek* in 2006: "I think we've
got to admit the possibility that we are not always right, that our
particular faith may not have all the monopoly on truth, and we've
got to be able to listen to other people … one of the trends … causing so much political grief both domestically and internationally, is
that absolutism has become sort of the flavor of the day."[28]

Sadly enough, absolutism has indeed become "the flavor of
the day." Sadly enough, absolutism has become the new political
agenda. Although first set in motion during the presidency of Ronald Reagan, absolutism, according to Barack Obama, would come

to take extreme forms under subsequent GOP presidents. The up-shot being, as Barack Obama strongly puts it, that "the ideological core of today's GOP is absolutism, not conservatism."[29] "Whatever the explanation," Barack Obama relates about these developments, "after Reagan the lines between Republican and Democrat, liberal and conservative, would be drawn in more sharply ideological terms. This was true, of course, for the hot-button issues of affirmative action, crime, welfare, abortion, and school prayer ... But it was also now true for every other issue, large or small, domestic or foreign, all of which were reduced to a menu of either-or, for-or-against, sound-bite-ready choices."[30]

Of course such ideological extremism only serves to widen the existing gap between that to which America aspires and that which she in fact is. But significantly this is not what Barack Obama finds most troubling about the new political absolutism. What he quite rightly finds most troubling is not that it serves to widen the gap between the aspirational and the actual, but rather, that it creates an unprecedented obstacle to overcoming that gap. Quite specifically, under the new absolutism, inclusivity gives way to exclusivity; the search for common solutions succumbs to chronic resistance and opposition; oversimplification mercilessly renders genuine problems meaningless, not to speak of proffered solutions; what needs to be embraced is avoided, especially the level of dialogue and process from which only truly functional solutions can issue. Describing the legislative gridlock characteristic of the new political absolutism, with reference to its implications for democratic process, Barack Obama relates,

> like most Americans, I find it hard to shake the feeling
> these days that our democracy has gone seriously awry.
>
> It's not simply that a gap exists between our pro-
> fessed ideals as a nation and the reality we witness every
> day. In one form or another, that gap has existed since
> America's birth. …
>
> No, what's troubling is the gap between the magni-
> tude of our challenges and the smallness of our politics …
> our debate on education seems stuck between those who
> want to dismantle the public school system and those who
> would defend an indefensible status quo … our health-
> care system is broken … But year after year, ideology and
> political gamesmanship result in inaction … follow most
> of our foreign policies debates, and you might believe that
> we have only two choices—belligerence or isolationism.
>
> We think of faith as a source of comfort and under-
> standing but find our expressions of faith sowing division;
> we believe ourselves to be a tolerant people even as racial,
> religious, and cultural tensions roil the landscape … in-
> stead of resolving these tensions … our politics … exploits
> them, and drives us further apart. … What's needed is a
> broad majority of Americans—Democrats, Republicans,
> and independents of goodwill—who are reengaged in the
> project of national renewal, and who see their own self-

interest as inextricably linked to the interests of others.[31]

It is perhaps not surprising that absolutistic assumptions about life and its meaning were not part of Barack Obama's own upbringing. In fact under his mother's direction, Barack Obama was led to view disparate and even competing religious belief systems and ideologies with empathic openness and tolerance, as he explained to Charlie Rose in an interview in 2006: "I didn't grow up in a religious household. My mother, who was an anthropologist, would take me to church once in a while, and then she would take me to the Buddhist monastery, and then she'd take me to a mosque. Her attitude was religion was fascinating and an expression of human attempts to understand the mysteries of life."[32] Of course the phrasing "human attempts to understand the mysteries of life" is not be overlooked, as it speaks, not to the possibility of an absolute understanding of the life process and God, but rather, to the possibility of an approximate understanding of the life process and God, much as is no less true of the limitations of scientific inquiry itself. Yet with such epistemological limitations and all her "professed secularism" taken into account, Barack Obama could only conclude about his mother that she "was in many ways the most spiritually awakened person that I've ever known. She had an unswerving instinct for kindness, charity, and love, and spent much of her life acting on that instinct, sometimes to her detriment … she worked mightily to instill in me the values that many Americans learn in Sunday school: honesty, empathy, discipline, delayed gratification, and hard work. She raged at poverty and injustice, and scorned those who were indifferent to both. Most of all, she possessed an abiding sense of wonder, a reverence for life and its precious, transitory nature that could properly be described as devotional."[33]

Whether we are speaking about secular or religious belief systems, the trajectory of fixed-form ideology is to impose on, rather than engage in process. Its trajectory is to ignore and override, rather than work with and work through. Its trajectory is to rise above and dominate, rather than meet and engage in process. Both openly and clandestinely, accordingly, fixed-form ideology proceeds, not by way of relatedness and meaning, not by way of dialogue and process, but rather, forcefully under the auspices of will and power. Speaking about this problem with reference to the damage inflicted on the American political process by the relentlessly pursued, ideological agenda of the Bush Administration, Barack Obama told the *New Yorker* in 2006: "This has been probably the most ideologically driven administration in my memory. And I don't know how far I'd have to go back to find one, a combination of a House, Senate, and White House, that has been so obstinate in resisting facts, dissenting opinions, compromise. Everything is based on a set of preconceived notions that ignore whatever reality and information comes at them. I think that this administration has done great damage to this country."[34]

The combination of fixed-form ideology with will and power, history has more than evidenced, makes for a most unholy synergy. Indeed to the extent fixed-form ideologies impose upon, rather than work with and through, dominate rather than engage in process, they necessarily compel those within their orbit to be far less conscious than they would otherwise be capable of being. Fixed-form ideologies lower the consciousness levels at which both individuals and groups function and in so doing they clear a path not only for oppression, but also, unconstrained abuse. Whether we are talking about secular or religious belief systems, the scourge of fixed-form ideologies is that under their cover power dynamics and pathologies obtain license to move freely and act with impunity. "For my mother," Barack Obama writes with reference to the religious expression of this problem, "organized religion too often dressed up closed-mindedness in the garb of piety, cruelty and oppression in the cloak of righteousness."[35] With reference to the secular or, more specifically, political expression of this problem in the form of "Bush's doctrine of preventive war," Barack Obama further relates:

> As the ouster of Saddam Hussein became the test case for Bush's doctrine of preventive war, those who questioned the Administration's rationale for invasion were accused of being 'soft on terrorism' or 'un-American.' Instead of an honest accounting of this military campaign's pros and cons, the Administration initiated a public relations offensive: shading intelligence reports to support its case, grossly understating both the costs and the manpower require-

ments of military action, raising the specter of mushroom clouds.

The PR strategy worked; by the fall of 2002, a majority of Americans were convinced that Saddam Hussein possessed weapons of mass destruction, and at least 66 percent believed (falsely) that the Iraqi leader had been personally involved in the 9/11 attacks. Support for an invasion of Iraq—and Bush's approval rating—hovered around 60 percent. With an eye on the midterm elections, Republicans stepped up the attacks and pushed for a vote authorizing the use of force against Saddam Hussein. And on October 11, 2002, twenty-eight of the Senate's fifty democrats joined all but one Republican in handing to Bush the power he wanted.[36]

It is nothing short of appalling that a nation would be seduced by ideologically-derived false absolutes and false certainties to the extent it would so quickly give its blessing to war and its horrific attendant costs, human, financial and moral; it is more disturbing still to consider for even a moment the subsequent suffering wrongly inflicted under the same pretenses on the targeted nation and its people.

Regardless of its military capability, regardless of its economic power, it is incumbent on a democratic nation never to succumb to the falsity and hubris that an imposed fixed-form ideological "solution" is equivalent to a truly ethical solution reached by way of process and sincere deliberation. The consciousness with which a nation holds the power in its possession is not only one of the most important measures of democratic culture, but no less of that nation's ethicality. Speaking before the United Nations in 1963, with reference to what he had quite rightly come to regard as the incontrovertible ethical responsibilities of the then two great superpowers, the United States and the Soviet Union, John Kennedy asserted: "The fact remains that the United States, as a major nuclear power, does have a special responsibility in the world. It is, in fact, a threefold responsibility—a responsibility to our own citizens; a responsibility to the people of the whole world who are affected by our decisions; and to the next generation of humanity. We believe the Soviet Union also has these special responsibilities."[37]

In contrast to the above, it is unfortunately the case ethicality typically succumbs to the base options power all too readily affords individuals and nations. Power corrupts individuals and nations precisely because it provides the means to impose on, rather than work with. Power corrupts because it allows individuals and nations to impose unreflectively and willfully on others without having to encounter in process the reality of the situation at hand. Power corrupts because it inflates the controlling ego causing it in turn to believe erroneously it has the power to make ideas, people, cultures, nations and even reality itself disappear without due process. In the big picture, however, nothing is further from the truth. Power corrupts because it gives license to unconsciousness, and in so doing it not only destroys the growth opportunity of the victim of such imposition, but no less the growth opportunity of the victimizer. Failure to engage an individual or nation in process, not only does the other individual or nation harm, but it no less does serious harm to oneself, for in both instances the precious opportunity to extend consciousness by way of self-organizing nature is altogether lost, corrupted.[38] Ethical leadership, by contrast, whether in international affairs, nationally or even within something as immediate as the dynamics of a family system, turns to engage in process that which it is not forced to engage; for ethical leadership knows that inclusivity and process are life's operant conditions. "I know, I have seen," Barack Obama writes in *Dreams from My Father*,

> the desperation and disorder of the powerless: how it twists the lives of children on the streets of Jakarta or Nairobi in much the same way as it does the lives of children on Chicago's South Side, how narrow the path is for them between humiliation and untrammeled fury, how easily they slip into violence and despair. I know that the response of the powerful to this disorder—alternating as it does between a dull complacency and, when the disorder spills out of its proscribed confines, a steady, unthinking application of force, of longer prison sentences and more sophisticated military hardware—is inadequate to the task. I know that the hardening of lines, the embrace of fundamentalism and tribe, dooms us all.[39]

Very much to the detriment of America, democratic culture and the world as a whole, the way of power has been the post-9/11 reality. Yet perhaps there now exists a glimmer of hope. Perhaps we are at a turning point. Perhaps it is the case that democratic culture's zealous pursuit of a false premise now stands exhausted and the folly of the way of power laid bare. "I think [Americans] instinctively understand," Barack Obama told the *Houston Chronicle* in 2006 with reference to the limitations of the way of power and ideological imposition, "that we cannot simply impose our will militarily on the entire globe."[40] Speaking even more directly to the post-9/11 moral failings and squandered leadership opportunities associated with America's current fixed ideological agenda operating under the auspices of an unprecedented military capability, Barack Obama told the Chicago Council on Foreign Relations in 2004: "American leadership has been a mighty force for human progress. ... Today we face new and frightful challenges, especially the threat of terror. Never has it been more important for America to lead wisely, to shrewdly project power and wield influence on behalf of liberty and security. Unfortunately, I fear our once great influence is waning, a victim of misguided policies and impetuous actions. Never has the U.S. possessed so much power, and never has the U.S. had so little influence to lead."[41]

The current and indeed urgent duty of America and democratic culture as a whole is to regain the ethical initiative. Perhaps at this moment in history, I will again say, with the folly of the way of power having been so fully exhausted in this post-9/11 period, we are ready to direct our energies toward that objective. Less than one month prior to his assassination, on the occasion of his tribute to the late poet Robert Frost at Amherst College on October 26, 1963, John Kennedy spoke of his vision for an ethical America, his vision for an ethical world: "I look forward to a great future for America, a future in which our country will match its military strength with our moral restraint, its wealth with our wisdom, its power with our purpose. I look forward to an America which will not be afraid of grace and beauty, which will protect the beauty of our natural environment ... I look forward to an America which commands respect throughout the world not only for its strength but for its civilization as well. And I look forward to a world which will be safe not only for democracy and diversity but also for personal distinction."[42]

All hope for a glorious future for not only democratic culture but for humanity as a whole, resides not in the way of power, not in concretized ideologies that confine and arrest the greatness of the human spirit by imposing arbitrary and false divisions between people and nations, but rather, with our individual and collective abilities to circumvent the walls of fixed-form ideologies. Along this very line, masterfully shifting consciousness from the exclusivity of the ideologically concretized to the inclusivity of the genuinely dynamic and living, Franklin Delano Roosevelt wrote, "Selfishness is the only real atheism; aspiration, unselfishness, the only real religion."[43]

The responsibility of individuals and nations must be to circumvent the walls of fixed-form ideology. It must be to extend consciousness beyond the limitations of ideological exclusivity and absolutism to inclusivity and process. It is especially the responsibility of democratic culture to work actively to achieve this, not only within and between democratic nations, but also in its dealings with all other nations. Every opportunity must be taken to circumvent ideological fixed forms so as to create the requisite space to engage and process the experiences, needs and aspirations of all those to whom we are bound by way of nature. In his capacity not only as an American president, but no less as a leader of democratic culture, John Kennedy quite rightly maintained that the attainment of world peace would require of nations a dialogue that would bring to the forefront, from behind the walls of ideological differences, the commonality of human experience in this process we call life. Ideological differences pale, Kennedy believed, when placed alongside the more primary definitions of who we are, what we would wish to become and what we would desire for others, especially those we love. "No government or social system is so evil," John Kennedy told his American University audience in seeking to direct their collective vision beyond the ideological walls separating the United States and the then Soviet Union, "that its people must be considered as lacking in virtue. ... So, let us not be blind to our differences—but let us also direct attention to our common interests and to the means by which those differences can be resolved. And if we cannot end now our differences, at least we can help make the world safe for diversity. For, in the final analysis, our most basic common link is that we all inhabit this small planet. We all breathe the same air. We all cherish our children's future. And we are all mortal."[44]

It is of no small significance to consider as a footnote to this section Barack Obama's comments to the people of Berlin and the world during his recent visit to that city. Of specific interest to our study is the manner in which he extended the meaning of a challenge that President Ronald Reagan had given to the then Soviet Union some twenty-one years previous. On June 12th, 1987, Ronald Reagan stood at the Brandenburg Gate in West Berlin and delivered in what was perhaps the most memorable speech of his presidency the following extraordinary challenge to the then General Secretary of the Soviet Union, Mikhail Gorbachev: "General Secretary Gorbachev, if you seek peace, if you seek prosperity for the Soviet Union and Eastern Europe, if you seek liberalization: Come here to this gate! Mr. Gorbachev, open this gate! Mr. Gorbachev, tear down this wall!"[45] On November 9th, 1989, what for Berliners, Europeans and the world had been the unimaginable, happened—the Berlin wall was breached with the consent of the East German government uniting a city that for over three decades had been divided. Speaking in July of 2008 to a Berlin throng of over 200,000, Barack Obama celebrated with the people of that city their great historical moment—the world's great historical moment. But he did not do so, it should be understood, without reference to the comparable exigencies of the present. He did not do so

without reference to the no less seemingly insurmountable walls
that to the great detriment of humanity needlessly divide and separate peoples and nations today. Of course the challenge to which
Barack Obama was referring is humanity's now urgent challenge
to breach the existing, yet no less seemingly insurmountable walls
of fixed-form ideologies. "People of the world," Barack Obama
offered,

> look at Berlin, where a wall came down, a continent came
> together, and history proved there is no challenge too great
> for a world that stands as one. ...
>
> Yes, there have been differences between America
> and Europe. ... But the burdens of global citizenship con-
> tinue to bind us together. ...
>
> That is why the greatest danger of all is to allow
> new walls to divide us from one another.
>
> The walls between old allies on either side of the
> Atlantic cannot stand. The walls between the countries
> with the most and those with the least cannot stand. The
> walls between races and tribes; natives and immigrants;
> Christian and Muslim and Jew cannot stand. These now
> are the walls we must tear down.[46]

III

A HUMAN BEING, FIRST AND FOREMOST

"When I meet people for the first time," Barack Obama related in *The Audacity of Hope,* "they sometimes quote back to me a line in my speech at the 2004 Democratic National Convention that seemed to strike a chord: 'There is not a black America and white America and Latino America and Asian America—there's the United States of America.' For them, it seems to capture a vision of America finally freed from the past of Jim Crow and slavery, Japanese internment camps and Mexican braceros, workplace tensions and cultural conflict—an America that fulfills Dr. King's promise that we be judged not by the color of our skin but by the content of our character."[47] Barack Obama is certainly not the first American politician to advocate passionately for the civil rights of all Americans. Yet there can be no doubt the words he spoke at the Democratic National Convention in 2004 resonated with the soul of America, not to speak of the soul of democratic culture as a whole, in a manner previous statements about ethnicity and race offered by others had not done. Yet why, we would ask, was this so? The answer to this question, I would offer, has to do with the fact that the vision for America of which Barack Obama spoke came from outside the box in which the discussion of ethnicity and race has typically been conducted. Quite specifically, the unique contribution of Barack Obama's 2004 convention speech was that it served to redirect attention from the conventional, yet ultimately polarizing focus on *equality/inequality in differences* to a point of view in which racial or ethnic differences are treated as ultimately secondary to the reality of the *fundamental sameness of all human beings*. Barack Obama did not say there is a black America and white America and Latino America and Asian America and they need to be equal. He said, rather, there is just one America, with just one people; there is just the United States of America. "The starting premise for me that my mother instilled in me, and my father inadvertently instilled," Barack Obama explained in a speech delivered at the Aspen Institute in July 2005, "was that everybody was the same."[48]

Now this shift from the *equality/inequality in differences* polarity to a focus on the *fundamental sameness of all human beings* could not have had a more profound effect on the 2004 Democratic Convention audience. But why, we would further wonder, were people who had never experienced ethnic or racial discrimination no less deeply touched than those who had? The answer has to do with the fact that as soon as we shift focus from the *equality/ inequality* polarity synonymous with matters of racial and ethnic justice to the issue of the *fundamental sameness of all human beings*, what to date has largely been a concern with two specific types of discrimination now gives way to the problem of discrimination in its multitudinous forms. Of course the reconfigured problem to which I am referring has to do with recognizing and overcoming the human propensity to deploy false absolutes against others. It has to do with recognizing and overcoming the human propensity to deploy false absolutes in any manner that would lessen or obstruct the engagement in process of an individual as a human being, first and foremost.

The impact of the above-described consciousness shift would have been such that there would not have been one individual at the Democratic convention to whom this now reconfigured problem of discrimination would not have directly spoken. Every single person who has lived on this earth has suffered at least one instance of the discriminatory imposition of a false absolute. Everyone has endured at least one instance of discriminatory labeling as a result of the imposition of a false absolute pertaining to race, ethnicity, sexual orientation, disability, gender, religion, age, physique, education, social or economic status, to name only but a few of the discriminatory possibilities. A brief reference to Paul Haggis' highly regarded film *Crash*, the recipient of the best film award of the 2006 Oscars, will help to extend this point.

Los Angeles, the city in which the film unfolds, is a metaphor for the disharmony and ultimate meaninglessness of modern-day existence. The modern world is indeed a world of exclusivity and separation; it is not a world of inclusivity and connection. The modern world is a world bereft of intimacy, either in the sense of meaningful relationship to others or self-relationship, which is to say, meaningful relationship to the unfolding process of one's own life. The modern world, in this regard, is a world in which people, being for the most part incapable of intimate encounter with each other and life in its glorious complexity, wander aimlessly in states of unrelatedness and alienation, not connecting to, but rather, *crashing* into each other.

Curiously enough, much as political pundits have wrongly sought to reduce Barack Obama's candidacy and message to the common denominator of race, the reviewers of Paul Haggis' *Crash* have been no less wrongly inclined to label the film an interracial drama. Clearly there can be no question that *Crash* speaks to the problem of racial and ethnic discrimination, but *Crash* certainly is not, on the other hand, limited to those themes. Yes, *Crash* presents numerous instances of interracial and interethnic tensions, but we no less observe in the film the operation and ultimate shattering of so many other discriminatory manifestations of false absolutes. We see interracial bashing and stereotyping, but we also see intraracial bashing and stereotyping, which is to say, people of the same race using stereotypes and false absolutes pertaining to their own race to demean each other. We see a mother who idealizes one son over another and doing so without any regard whatsoever for their respective behaviors. We see "good guys" who in reality are "bad guys"; we see those who have been violators of others turn into heroes, even to the extent of placing themselves at risk of death. *Crash*, we should just say, is much more than an interracial drama.

The problem *Crash* holds out to us and attempts to bring to consciousness is the problem of the psychopathology of our everyday lives as viewed against the backdrop of the inclusive dynamics of self-organizing nature. Much to our own detriment and to the detriment of those within our everyday orbit, we go about our lives largely under the influence of false absolutes. Now although such false absolutes distort and even degrade our experiences of each other and life, the self-organizing process that life is in its essence is in no way subject to such limitations. The self-organizing direction of nature, accordingly, in spite of our unconsciousness and resistance to growth, in spite of the biases and prejudices to which we so desperately cling, is that our experience and understanding of people and life should be altogether freed from illusory obstructions. The direction of self-organizing nature is that by way of emergent pattern the meaning concealed from our everyday gaze by the illusory workings of false absolutes should be revealed to us. Los Angeles, the City of Angels, *Crash* thus tells us, is the place, as with all cities, towns and villages, where the self-organizing process that life is reaches through our everyday encounters, through the illusions cast by false absolutes in their myriad forms, to reveal itself to us.

A world in which people are first and foremost categorized and engaged along the arbitrary lines of race and ethnicity; a world in which people are first and foremost categorized and engaged along the lines of age, gender, religious belief or lack thereof, sexual orientation, social and economic status; a world in which people are labeled without justification "good guys" or "bad guys," patriotic or unpatriotic; a world in which other nations are conceived of as absolutely good or absolutely evil is a dehumanizing world indeed. To dehumanize by way of the imposition of false absolutes is to license the engagement of others through power. To license the engagement of others through power is in effect to license disengagement.

Human beings, as already explained, have a fundamental need for certainty, but seldom do they undertake the requisite work to come to it by way of truth and meaning. The resultant experience, accordingly, is more accurately termed false certainty. False absolutes are no substitutes for truth and meaning, much as false certainty is but a parody of a conviction whose ground is self-organizing nature. False absolutes and false certainties never satiate an altogether healthy need for depth meaning, but rather, merely provisionally appease an ultimately insatiable and altogether unhealthy need for control. Yet this being so, people nonetheless persevere undeterred in their vain attempts to manipulate and control reality. People nonetheless persevere undeterred in their search for yet another false absolute by which they might raise themselves up or push others down. People nonetheless persevere undeterred in search of yet another false absolute by which they might lessen or altogether obstruct their engagement with another individual as a human being, first and foremost. In his highly regarded speech on race, Barack Obama spoke frankly about his own catch-22-like

experience of being the recipient of what we would here term projected false absolutes when he stated: "At various stages in the
campaign, some commentators have deemed me either 'too black'
or 'not black enough.'"[49] Describing elsewhere his personal aversion to such absolutistic categorizations, he explains: "I've always
been clear that I'm rooted in the African-American community but
not limited to it."[50]

In his celebrated sermon "The Drum Major Instinct," Martin Luther King, drawing on the personality theorist Alfred Adler's
belief in the human drive for superiority, told the congregants at
Atlanta's Ebenezer Baptist Church: "… there is deep down within
all of us an instinct. It's a kind of drum major instinct—a desire to
be out front, a desire to lead the parade, a desire to be first."[51] There
are, Martin Luther King went on to tell those in attendance, not just
healthy manifestations of this instinct, but unhealthy ones as well,
perhaps the most pernicious of which being, to use the language of
this study, the tendency to use false absolutes to create illusions of
superiority. "Do you know," Martin Luther King explained with
reference to the instinct's unhealthy manifestations, "that a lot of
the race problem grows out of the drum major instinct? A need
that some people have to feel superior. A need that some people
have to feel that they are first, and to feel that their white skin or-
dained them to be first."[52] Do you know, I would further add, that
a lot of the race problems and ethnic tensions that exist between all
the peoples of the world are attributable to the similar deployment
of false absolutes to elevate one race or one ethnic group over an-

other? Do you know, moreover, to the extent an individual would be drawn into an illusion of exclusivity by way of identification with a false absolute, such a person would not only be incapable of recognizing and engaging the needs and experiences of others, but would be equally incapable of recognizing and engaging his or her own needs and experiences? The deployment of a false absolute, in this regard, would not only obstruct one's engagement of another individual as a human being, first and foremost, but it no less would obstruct one's engagement of oneself as a human being, first and foremost. Self-elevation and exclusivity by way of identification with a false absolute, we can thus conclude, is not even in one's own best interest. Using the events associated with one of his more than twenty jailings[53] to make a comparable point, Martin Luther King, told his Ebenezer Baptist Church congregates:

> The other day I was saying, I always try to do a little converting when I'm in jail. And when we were in jail in Birmingham the other day, the white wardens and all enjoyed coming around the cell to talk about the race problem. And they were showing us where we were so wrong demonstrating. And they were showing us where segregation was so right. And they were showing us where intermarriage was so wrong. So I would get to preaching, and we would get to talking— calmly, because they wanted to talk about it. And then we got down one day to the point— that was the second or third day—to talk about where they

lived, and how much they were earning. And when those brothers told me what they were earning, I said, 'Now, you know what? You ought to be marching with us. [*laughter*] You're just as poor as Negroes.' And I said, 'You are put in the position of supporting your oppressor, because through prejudice and blindness, you fail to see that the same forces that oppress Negroes in American society oppress poor white people. (*Yes*) And all you are living on is the satisfaction of your skin being white, and the drum major instinct of thinking that you are somebody big because you are white. And you're so poor you can't send your children to school. You ought to be out here marching with every one of us every time we have a march.'

Now that's a fact. That the poor white has been put into this position, where through blindness and prejudice, (*Make it plain*) he is forced to support his oppressors. And the only thing he has going for him is the false feeling that he's superior because his skin is white—and can't hardly eat and make his ends meet week in and week out. (*Amen*)[54]

Self-elevation and exclusivity by way of identification with a false absolute, I will again say, not only renders individuals incapable of recognizing and engaging the needs and experiences of others, but no less renders individuals incapable of recognizing and engaging their own needs and experiences. If we are to allow

the fabricated exclusivity of a false absolute to keep us from identifying with the experiences and lives of others, if we are to allow
false absolutes associated with race, ethnicity, age, gender, sexual
orientation, disability, religious belief or lack thereof to keep us
from seeing ourselves in the problems we in fact have in common
with others, how will we as a culture harness the requisite energy,
strength and collective will to find our way to genuine solutions?

If we are truly to embrace change, all false certainties, all
those things to which we cling that would arbitrarily and falsely
separate us from each other and life must be surrendered. Even an
experience of victimization, we should understand, can become a
false absolute—a false absolute of exclusivity. Victimization can
indeed become a false absolute to the extent it is deployed to de-
fend or excuse an individual or people from encountering life in
process as it presents in the here and now. Victimization can become a false absolute to the extent it is held so firmly it altogether
precludes an individual or people, who are developmentally ready
and needing to move on, from so doing. As much, therefore, as the
illusion of exclusivity attending the false absolute of *being better
than* will developmentally arrest an individual by suppressing the
fact of one's experiences of hardship and suffering, the illusion of
exclusivity attending the false absolute of *being the victim of* will in
equal measure developmentally arrest an individual by suppressing the actuality of one's strengths. Speaking with reference to the
need to ensure the appalling history of African-American victimization does not become a false absolute in its own right, which is

to say, the victimized becoming victims only, speaking, moreover, with reference to the need to ensure false absolutes of racial exclusivity do not prevent the American people seeing and addressing collectively the genuine needs and aspirations of each and every American, Barack Obama explained in his speech on race:

> Contrary to the claims of some of my critics, black and white, I have never been so naive as to believe that we can get beyond our racial divisions in a single election cycle, or with a single candidacy—particularly a candidacy as imperfect as my own.
>
> But I have asserted a firm conviction—a conviction rooted in my faith in God and my faith in the American people—that working together we can move beyond some of our old racial wounds, and that in fact we have no choice if we are to continue on the path of a more perfect union.
>
> For the African-American community, that path means embracing the burdens of our past without becoming victims of our past. It means continuing to insist on a full measure of justice in every aspect of American life. But it also means binding our particular grievances—for better health care, and better schools and better jobs—to the larger aspirations of all Americans—the white woman struggling to break the glass ceiling, the white man who's been laid off, the immigrant trying to feed his family. And it means taking full responsibility for [our] own lives—by

demanding more from our fathers, and spending more time with our children, and reading to them, and teaching them that while they may face challenges and discrimination in their own lives, they must never succumb to despair or cynicism; they must always believe that they can write their own destiny.[55]

A world in which human beings categorize themselves or categorize others, first and foremost, in terms of false absolutes pertaining to race, ethnicity, age, disability, gender, religious belief or lack thereof, sexual orientation, social and economic status; a world in which people without just cause are deemed "good guys" or "bad guys," patriotic or unpatriotic; a world in which other nations are conceived of as absolutely good or absolutely evil is a dehumanizing world indeed. People dehumanize themselves, as we have just seen, to the extent they construct by way of false absolutes illusory notions of exclusivity and superiority; people dehumanize others, as we shall now more fully understand, to the extent they deprive others by way of false absolutes of the right to be viewed as human beings, first and foremost. Of course at the farthest end of this particular continuum would be the demonization of others by way of the assignment of labels the collective has either explicitly or implicitly accepted to designate as much.

People typically honor the rights of those whom they look upon as the same as themselves; conversely, they do not extend rights to those upon whom they have conferred subhuman status, which is to say, those whom they have demonized. The deployment of false absolutes to label individuals or nations as categorically evil, it should thus be understood, amounts to nothing less than the fastest route to becoming truly evil ourselves. Was not the post-9/11 war on terror announced to the world as essentially a war against evil, the axis of evil, to be sure, and where has that taken democratic culture? Have the actions of democratic governments in the ensuing years not triggered unprecedented concerns about violations of international law and human rights? Has history not unequivocally demonstrated that the demonization of others has offered democratic culture nothing more than justification for conduct unbecoming of its true values? Has history not unequivocally demonstrated that demonization has done no more than give license to the unethical and illegal treatment of others? Has history not more than demonstrated that the legacy of demonization, although powerfully driven by human passions and embraced under the circumstances of a given time, has never amounted to something of which we are proud in the long run? How could it? For once fear-driven passions have subsided that which history holds out to us no longer presents as cleansings and necessary self-protective measures, but rather, as witch-hunts, lynch-mob justice, McCarthyism, racial profiling, unwarranted and even illegal war, incarceration and prosecution without due process, harassment, torture, murder and even genocide.

The imposition of a false absolute to the extent it would present an everyday and on-going obstruction to the acceptance of an individual as a human being, first and foremost, is typically an experience to which the majority of citizens in a given democratic nation have not been exposed. The majority of citizens do not know what it is like to have a demeaning projection coming at them each and every day. They do not know what it is like to live with an ongoing projection that has at every turn the potential to override their identities as human beings, first and foremost. And indeed the fact they do not explains why democratic nations, acting under even the best of intentions, are more than challenged to hold consciousness on the civil rights plight of their minorities, especially their visible minorities.

The majority of people, to be sure, do not know what it is like to be the recipient of a continuous, demeaning projection, but there are rare occasions when those for whom this is typically not their experience are given a glimpse of what it actually feels like to be on the wrong side of a collectively projected false absolute. It is not a good place to be, especially when you are not used to it, just ask the Dixie Chicks.

It is well-known the Dixie Chicks' initiatory step into this dehumanizing space occurred just prior to the Iraq invasion in 2003 when Natalie Maines told their London, England audience: "Just so you know, we're ashamed the President of the United States is from Texas."[56] What ensued was perhaps best summed up by fellow country-western music star Merle Haggard, who likened the ordeal to which the women were subjected to "'a verbal witch-hunt and lynching.'" In an essay posted on his website, Haggard wrote:

"'I don't even know the Dixie Chicks, but I find it an insult for all men and women who fought and died in past wars when almost the majority of America jumped down their throats for voicing an opinion. It was like a verbal witch-hunt and lynching.'"[57] For their part, the Dixie Chicks encapsulated the shock and incredulity attending their encounter with dehumanization by way of collective projection when they wrote in their song *Not Ready to Make Nice*: "It's a sad sad story when a mother will teach her/Daughter that she ought to hate a perfect stranger/And how in the world can the words that I said/Send somebody so over the edge/That they'd write me a letter/Sayin' that I better shut up and sing/Or my life will be over."[58] A documentary film on these events, directed by two-time Oscar-winner Barbara Kopple and Cecilia Peck titled *Shut Up and Sing* is fittingly subtitled: *Freedom of speech is fine as long as you don't do it in public.*[59]

Although individual rights and freedoms within democratic countries are typically enshrined constitutionally, the manner in which they are held in consciousness at ground level in the practical realities of the day-to-day is of no small significance to democratic culture. It should be recalled from the above that at a critical moment in the civil rights struggle, John Kennedy adamantly directed his fellow Americans as follows: "In too many of our cities today, the peace is not secure because freedom is incomplete. It is the responsibility of the executive branch at all levels of government—local, State and National—to provide and protect that freedom for all of our citizens by all means within their authority. It is the responsibility of the legislative branch at all levels, wherever that authority is not now adequate, to make it adequate. And it is the responsibility of all citizens in all sections of this country to respect the rights of all others and to respect the law of the land." Of course it is John Kennedy's last directive with which we are especially concerned, where he speaks to the problem of ensuring rights and freedoms for all Americans by way of all Americans—where he speaks to the need for all Americans to accept as their duty the responsibility of ensuring the rights and freedoms of each and every American at ground level in the practical realities of the day-to-day.

The honoring of individual rights and freedoms in the practical realities of the day-to-day means everything to the functionality of democratic process, not to speak of the integrity of democratic culture itself. Yet how, we would ask, with the concerns of this section in mind, can we keep false absolutes from coming into play within the collective consciousness in a manner that would compromise freedom of expression, especially where freedom of expression is tested in the forms of *dissent* or *diversity*? How, we would further ask, can we keep false absolutes from coming into play within the collective consciousness to the extent they would compromise individual rights and freedoms, especially the most basic right to be treated as a human being, first and foremost?

The problem with which we are faced is that by way of false absolutes *dissent* and *diversity* are readily demonized. Concerning the question of dissent, we saw what a mere sentence of opposition in the case of the Dixie Chicks unleashed; concerning the question of diversity, we could take as our case in point the controversy surrounding Barack Obama's flag lapel pin or lack thereof.

It is a curious fact that although the majority of candidates for both political parties during the primaries chose not to wear a flag lapel pin with any degree of consistency, Barack Obama was the one whose patriotism was directly called into question for not doing so. As *ABC News* reported: "Democrat John Edwards almost always wears his late son's Outward Bound pin. Hillary Clinton tends not to wear the flag pin … Her husband, former President Bill Clinton, wears a Hillary pin."[60] As *Time* related: "The only G.O.P. candidate to wear the pin faithfully was Rudy Giuliani. Is it fair that Obama is singled out for pin scrutiny? Probably not."[61] Which begs the rhetorical question: So why was he?

Something that should be understood about the term diversity, as I am here using it, is that it denotes nothing more than a preference to do something in a different way than others would choose to do it. Diversity, however, as we know, is cast in an altogether different light once false absolutes are brought into play. For example, as a result of the activation of false absolutes pertaining to patriotism, Barack Obama's personal preference not to wear the flag lapel pin each and every day was wrongly construed as a rejection of the flag pin and all that it stood for. Some went even further to see his personal preference as a rejection of the American flag itself—even though this preference, I will again note, was exercised by other candidates without the same conclusions being drawn.

The truth is that Barack Obama was not rejecting the wearing of the flag lapel pin as such. What Barack Obama was rejecting was its presentation as a *necessary* symbol of one's patriotism, which is to say, its conversion into a false absolute—a conversion which, Barack Obama would also hold, could do no more than create the potential for an otherwise revered American symbol to be abused by others to create but illusions of patriotism. "'After a while,'" Barack Obama explains, "'you start noticing people wearing a lapel pin, but not acting very patriotic. Not voting to provide veterans with resources that they need. Not voting to make sure that disability payments were coming out on time ... My attitude is that I'm less concerned about what you're wearing on your lapel than what's in your heart.'"[62]

It thus becomes apparent that finding our way forward has to do with rethinking the key word in the equation, which is the word *patriotism*. It has to do with the fact false absolutes wrongly reduce life to the one-dimensional when life is complex and multi-dimensional. It has to do with, shall we just say, giving the word patriotism multi-dimensionality.

In contrast to the assumptions of the politically and culturally one-dimensional, within the highly complex dynamics of democratic process, patriotism takes the form of neither absolute conformity nor absolute uniformity. Accordingly, in contrast to the blind adherence so characteristic of the false-absolutistic version of patriotism, those who truly stand on guard for democratic culture will be those who care enough and have the courage to question and challenge its social and political directions when it is required of them by their intelligence, feelings and conscience to do so.

What relationship would be worthy of such a designation that would amount to no more than blind or mindless adherence by either party? Relationship is a dynamic interactive process in which genuine, meaningful and energetic input needs to be offered and received by all stakeholders. No household would be considered functional if that were not the case; no marriage would be considered functional if that were not the case; no business partnership would be considered functional if that were not the case; no parent/child relationship would be considered functional if that were not the case. So how could a democracy that exists not as an ideal, but in its true form as a self-organizing process, be considered functional if it were not a dynamic, interactive process in which genuine, meaningful and energetic input is offered and received by all stakeholders?

Patriotism is not about blind and unthinking adherence to the current political agenda of one's nation; patriotism, rather, is about caring enough to engage intelligently and passionately and in turn progress the functionality of the values, beliefs, rights, freedoms, judicial and democratic processes that are the foundational heart and soul of one's nation and by extension democratic culture. Such patriotism, accordingly, as the above section on false absolutes and ideals has prepared us to understand, places an especially great burden on those to whom their nation's imperfections are most evident. "Mainstream America," Reverend Dr. Michael Eric Dyson wrote in April of 2008 with reference to this very dilemma,

> has shown little understanding lately of the patriotism that a lot of black people practice. Black love of country is often far more robust and complicated than the lapel-pin nationalism some citizens swear by. Barack Obama hinted at this when he declared in Montana a few weeks ago, 'I love this country not because it's perfect but because we've always been able to move it closer to perfection.' ...
>
> That's a far cry from the 'My country, right or wrong' credo, which confuses blind boosterism with a more authentic, if sometimes questioning, loyalty. At their best, black folk offer critical patriotism, an exacting devotion that carries on a lover's quarrel with America while they shed blood in its defense.[63]

For democratic culture to find its way beyond the concrete, one-dimensional world of false absolutes into the highly dynamic, multi-dimensional world of complex process, the voices and experiences of dissent and diversity must be more than grudgingly received. Dissent and diversity are not the optional accessories of democratic process and democratic culture, rather, they are the *sine qua non*—the *without which not* of its functional existence.

One-dimensionality may be the profile of the world of

false absolutes, but it is not the profile of reality. One-dimensionality may be the profile of the world of false absolutes, but it is not the true profile of democratic nations within the new world order of globalization. Not the one-dimensional, but rather, the multi-dimensional stands as the yet to be acknowledged actuality of all nations in both their internal and external affairs. Diversity, dissent, inclusivity, process, pluralism, complexity and multi-dimensionality are no longer the exceptions, but rather, the new order of the day.

Within the chaos of complex global dynamics, I would offer by way of closing, the only true, incontrovertible point of reference for democratic culture and the world as a whole is the human being. No matter what hemisphere, no matter what continent, no matter what country or nation, no matter what city, no matter what town or village, the only true point of reference in this our diverse, pluralistic, multi-dimensional world is to be found in the experience of the individual human being, as a human being, first and foremost, unencumbered by false absolutes, in self-organizing process.

NOTES

1. Robert Aziz, *The Syndetic Paradigm: The Untrodden Path Beyond Freud and Jung* (Albany, NY: State University of New York Press, 2007).

2. Lisa Rogak, ed., *Barack Obama In His Own Words* (New York: Carroll & Graf, 2007), 97.

3. Ibid., 148.

4. Barack Obama, "Remarks of Senator Barack Obama: Iowa Jefferson-Jackson Dinner" (speech in Des Moines, IA, November 10, 2007): http://www.barackobama.com/2007/11/10/remarks_of_senator_barack_obam_33.php.

5. Barack Obama, *The Audacity of Hope: Thoughts on Reclaiming the American Dream* (New York: Crown Publishers, 2006), 116.

6. Aziz, *The Syndetic Paradigm*, 288.

7. Caroline Kennedy, "Endorsement of Barack Obama" (remarks at American University, Washington, DC, January 28, 2008): http://blog.4president.org/2008/2008/01/senator-edwar-1.html.

8. John F. Kennedy, "Commencement Address at American University" (speech at American University, Washington, DC, June 10, 1963): http://www.jfklibrary.org/Historical+Resources/Archives/Reference+Desk/Speeches/JFK/003POF03American University06101963.htm.

9. Obama, *The Audacity of Hope*, 31-32.

10. Ibid., 33-34.

11. Kennedy, "Commencement Address at American University."

12. Franklin D. Roosevelt, "Democracy cannot succeed...," (eNotes.com.2006): http://www.enotes.com/famous-quotes/democracy-cannot-succeed-unless-those-who-express.

13. Aziz, *The Syndetic Paradigm*, 244-245.

14. Martin Luther King, Jr., "The Drum Major Instinct" (sermon delivered at Ebenezer Baptist Church, Atlanta, GA, February 4, 1968): http://www.stanford.edu/group/king/publications/sermons/680204.000_Drum_Major_Instinct.html.

15. C. G. Jung, ed., *Man and His Symbols* (Garden City, NJ: Doubleday & Company, Inc., 1979), 85.

16. Kennedy, "Commencement Address at American University."

17. Thomas Merton, *Contemplative Prayer* (New York: Image Books Doubleday, 1996), 103-104.

18. Lao Tsu, *Tao Te Ching*, trans. J. Legge (1891): http://www.sacred-texts.com/tao/taote.htm.

19. Lao Tsu, *Tao Te Ching*, trans. Gia-fu Feng and Jane English (New York: Vintage, 1972), no. 69.

20. Obama, *The Audacity of Hope*, 286.

21. Kennedy, "Commencement Address at American University."

22. Jimmy Carter, *Palestine Peace Not Apartheid* (New York: Simon & Schuster Paperbacks, 2007), 15-16.

23. John F. Kennedy, "Address Before the 18th General Assembly of the United Nations" (speech in New York, September 20, 1963): http://www.jfklibrary.org/Historical+Resources/Archives/Reference+Desk/Speeches/JFK/003POF03_18thGeneral Assembly09201963.htm.

24. Obama, *The Audacity of Hope*, 314-315.

25. Rogak, ed., *Barack Obama In His Own Words*, 105.

26. Aziz, *The Syndetic Paradigm*, 292-293.

27. Ibid., 289.

28. Rogak, ed., *Barack Obama In His Own Words*, 138.

29. Obama, *The Audacity of Hope*, 37.

30. Ibid., 32-33.

31. Ibid., 22-23 and 40.

32. Rogak, ed., *Barack Obama In His Own Words*, 137.

33. Obama, *The Audacity of Hope*, 205.

34. Rogak, ed., *Barack Obama In His Own Words*, 129.

35. Obama, *The Audacity of Hope*, 203.

36. Ibid., 293.

37. Kennedy, "Address Before the 18th General Assembly of the United Nations."

38. Robert Aziz, "Why Power Corrupts and Absolute Power Corrupts Absolutely": http://www.robertaziz.com/business_consulting/why_power_corrupts_and_absolut.php#more.

39. Barack Obama, *Dreams From My Father: A Story of Race and Inheritance* (New York: Crown Publishers, 2004), x-xi.

40. Rogak, ed., *Barack Obama In His Own Words*, 47.

41. Ibid., 45.

42. John F. Kennedy, "Remarks at Amherst College" (speech at Amherst College, Massachusetts, October, 26, 1963): http://www.jfklibrary.org/Historical+Resources/Archives/Reference+Desk/Speeches/JFK/003POF03Amherst10261963.htm.

43. Franklin D. Roosevelt, "Selfishness is the only real atheism...,": http://www.thinkexist.com/English/Author/x/Author_2884_5.htm.

44. Kennedy, "Commencement Address at American University."

45. Ronald Reagan, "Tear Down this Wall" (remarks at the Brandenburg Gate, West Berlin, Germany, June 12, 1987): http://www.reaganlibrary.com/reagan/speeches/speech.asp?spid=25.

46. Barack Obama, "Remarks of Senator Barack Obama: A World that Stands as One" (speech in Berlin, Germany, July 24, 2008): http://www.barackobama.com/2008/07/24/remarks_of_senator_barack_obam_97.php.

47. Obama, *The Audacity of Hope*, 231.

48. Rogak, ed., *Barack Obama In His Own Words*, 95.

49. Barack Obama, "Remarks of Senator Barack Obama: 'A More Perfect Union'" (speech in Philadelphia. PA, March 18, 2008): http://www.barackobama.com/2008/03/18/remarks_of_senator_barack_obam_53.php.

50. Rogak, ed., *Barack Obama In His Own Words*, 95.

51. Martin Luther King, Jr., "The Drum Major Instinct."

52. Ibid.

53. Nobelprize.org: http://nobelprize.org/nobel_prizes/peace/laureates/1964/king-bio.html.

54. Martin Luther King, Jr., "The Drum Major Instinct."

55. Barack Obama, "Remarks of Senator Barack Obama: 'A More Perfect Union.'"

56. "Dixie Chicks Slammed For Bush Gibe," *CBS News* (March 14, 2003): http://www.cbsnews.com/stories/2003/03/15/entertainment/main544132.shtml?source=search_story.

57. "Merle Haggard Sounds Off," *CBS News* (July 25, 2003): http://www.cbsnews.com/stories/2003/07/25/entertainment/main565038.shtml?source=search_story.

58. Dixie Chicks, "Not Ready to Make Nice," *Taking The Long Way*, Sony BMG Music Entertainment compact disc.

59. "Shut Up and Sing," *The Internet Movie Database*: http://www.imdb.com/title/tt0811136/.

60. David Wright and Sunlen Miller, "Obama Dropped Flag Pin in War Statement," *ABC News* (October 4, 2007): http://abcnews.go.com/print?id=3690000.

61. Jay Newton-Small, "Obama's Flag Pin Flip-Flop?," *Time* (May 14, 2008): http://www.time.com/time/politics/article/0,8599,1779544,00.html.

62. Ibid.

63. Michael Eric Dyson, "Understanding Black Patriotism," *Time* (April 24, 2008): http://www.time.com/time/magazine/article/0,9171,1734809.00.html.

BIBLIOGRAPHY

Aziz, Robert. *The Syndetic Paradigm: The Untrodden Path Beyond Freud and Jung.* Albany, NY: State University of New York Press, 2007.

Aziz, Robert. "Why Power Corrupts and Absolute Power Corrupts Absolutely.": http://www.robertaziz.com/business_consulting/why_power_corrupts_and_absolut.php#more.

Carter, Jimmy. *Palestine Peace Not Apartheid.* New York: Simon & Schuster Paperbacks, 2007.

Dixie Chicks. "Not Ready to Make Nice." *Taking The Long Way.* Sony BMG Music Entertainment compact disc.

"Dixie Chicks Slammed For Bush Gibe." *CBS News*, March 14, 2003: http://www.cbsnews.com/stories/2003/03/15/entertainment/main544132.shtml?source=search_story.

Dyson, Michael Eric. "Understanding Black Patriotism." *Time*, April 24, 2008: http://www.time.com/time/magazine/article/0,9171,1734809.00.html.

Jung, C. G., ed. *Man and His Symbols.* Garden City, NJ: Doubleday & Company, Inc., 1979.

Kennedy, Caroline. "Endorsement of Barack Obama." Remarks
    at American University, Washington, DC, January 28,
    2008: http://blog.4president.org/2008/2008/01/senator-
    edwar-1.html.

Kennedy, John F. "Address Before the 18th General Assembly of
    the United Nations." Speech in New York, September 20,
    1963: http://www.jfklibrary.org/Historical+Resources/
    Archives/Reference+Desk/Speeches/JFK/003POF03_
    18thGeneralAssembly09201963.htm.

Kennedy, John F. "Commencement Address at American
    University." Speech at American University, Washington,
    DC, June 10, 1963: http://www.jfklibrary.org/
    Historical+Resources/Archives/Reference+Desk/
    Speeches/JFK/003POF03AmericanUniversity06101963.
    htm.

Kennedy, John F. "Remarks at Amherst College." Speech at
    Amherst College, Massachusetts, October, 26, 1963:
    http://www.jfklibrary.org/Historical+Resources/
    Archives/Reference+Desk/Speeches/
    JFK/003POF03Amherst10261963.htm.

King, Jr., Martin Luther. "The Drum Major Instinct." Sermon
    delivered at Ebenezer Baptist Church, Atlanta, GA,
    February 4, 1968: http://www.stanford.edu/group/
    king/publications/sermons/680204.000_Drum_Major_
    Instinct.html.

Lao Tsu. *Tao Te Ching.* Translated by Gia-fu Feng and Jane English. New York: Vintage, 1972.

Lao Tsu. *Tao Te Ching.* Translated by J. Legge (1891): http://www.sacred-texts.com/tao/taote.htm.

"Merle Haggard Sounds Off." *CBS News,* July 25, 2003: http://www.cbsnews.com/stories/2003/07/25/entertainment/main565038.shtml?source=search_story.

Merton, Thomas. *Contemplative Prayer.* New York: Image Books Doubleday, 1996.

Newton-Small, Jay. "Obama's Flag Pin Flip-Flop?" *Time,* May 14, 2008: http://www.time.com/time/politics/article/0,8599,1779544,00.html.

Nobelprize.org: http://nobelprize.org/nobel_prizes/peace/laureates/1964/king-bio.html.

Obama, Barack. *Dreams From My Father: A Story of Race and Inheritance.* New York: Crown Publishers, 2004.

Obama, Barack. "Remarks of Senator Barack Obama: 'A More Perfect Union.'" Speech in Philadelphia, PA. March 18, 2008: http://www.barackobama.com/2008/03/18/remarks_of_senator_barack_obam_53.php.

Obama, Barack. "Remarks of Senator Barack Obama: A World that Stands as One." Speech in Berlin, Germany, July 24, 2008: http://www.barackobama.com/2008/07/24/remarks_of_senator_barack_obam_97.php.

Obama, Barack. "Remarks of Senator Barack Obama: Iowa
    Jefferson-Jackson Dinner." Speech in Des Moines,
    IA, November 10, 2007: http://www.barackobama.
    com/2007/11/10/remarks_of_senator_barack_obam_33.
    php.

Obama, Barack. *The Audacity of Hope: Thoughts on Reclaiming the
    American Dream*. New York: Crown Publishers, 2006.

Reagan, Ronald. "Tear Down this Wall." Remarks at the
    Brandenburg Gate, West Berlin, Germany, June 12, 1987:
    http://www.reaganlibrary.com/reagan/speeches/
    speech.asp?spid=25.

Rogak, Lisa, ed. *Barack Obama In His Own Words*. New York:
    Carroll & Graf, 2007.

Roosevelt, Franklin D. "Democracy cannot succeed... ." eNotes.
    com.2006: http://www.enotes.com/famous-quotes/
    democracy-cannot-succeed-unless-those-who-express.

Roosevelt, Franklin D. "Selfishness is the only real atheism....":
    http://www.thinkexist.com/English/Author/x/
    Author_2884_5.htm.

"Shut Up and Sing." *The Internet Movie Database*: http://www.
    imdb.com/title/tt0811136/.

Wright, David and Sunlen Miller. "Obama Dropped Flag Pin
    in War Statement." *ABC News*, October 4, 2007: http://
    abcnews.go.com/print?id=3690000.

www.ingramcontent.com/pod-product-compliance
Lightning Source LLC
Chambersburg PA
CBHW060639290526
45793CB00001B/315